AMERICA'S HEROES

TRIUMPH
BOOKS

Library of Congress Cataloguing-in-Publication Data available upon request

This book is available in quantity at special discounts for your group or organization. For further information, contact:
Triumph Books LLC
814 North Franklin Street
Chicago, Illinois 60610
(312) 337-0747
www.triumphbooks.com

Printed in U.S.A.
ISBN: 978-1-62937-858-9

Content written, developed, and packaged by Adam Motin
Design and page production by Patricia Frey
Cover design by Preston Pisellini

All photos courtesy of Getty Images unless otherwise indicated
Title page photo courtesy of AP Images

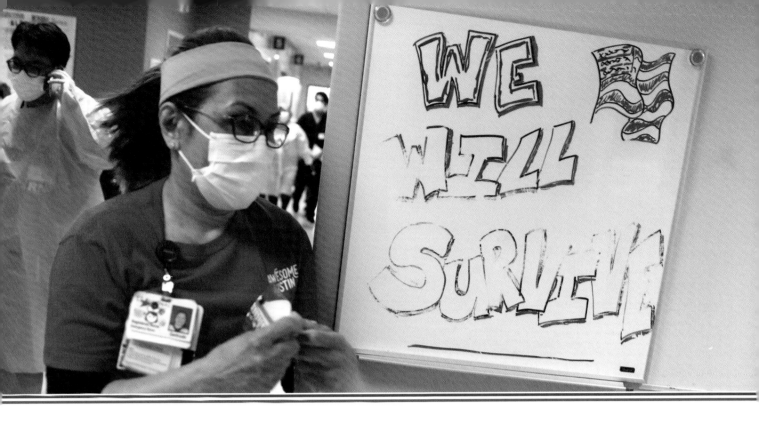

Contents

A medical worker poses for a portrait outside NYU Langone Hospital in New York City.

Introduction

America is no stranger to adversity. Throughout our history, our mettle has been tested in ways big and small, by unpredictable events beyond our control and during crises of our own making. Wars, both at home and abroad. Natural disasters. Economic depressions. Struggles for equality. For nearly 350 years, the only constant in our lives has been change.

Though these events may have been unrelated, they were all met with the same unstoppable force: the spirit and fortitude of the American people.

In 2020, we faced a challenge unlike almost any in human history: the Covid-19 global pandemic. The infectious disease, first identified in late 2019, quickly spread to nearly 200 countries, afflicting millions of people and killing hundreds of thousands. Practically overnight, our daily lives turned unrecognizable. Businesses of all kinds, schools, and places of worship were closed. Millions of Americans were left unemployed. Doctors and hospitals warned of being completely overwhelmed by those suffering from the disease. Government struggled to contain the scale of the chaos. What seemed unimaginable one day—wearing masks, separating ourselves from our loved ones, shuttering entire sectors of our economy—had become commonplace the next.

Fortunately, when called to action, the American people responded once again.

Medical professionals worked around the clock in makeshift facilities, putting their own lives and those of their families at risk, to battle a virus they knew little about. While millions were directed to stay home, millions more continued to work in essential industries, delivering products and other critical services. Everyday Americans, desperate to do their part, sprang into motion, making homemade masks, organizing food banks, and supporting those on the front lines. The most famous among us, such as celebrities and athletes, used their platforms to raise money and awareness for the cause.

The following pages celebrate the indomitable spirit of our American heroes, proving once more that there is no problem we cannot solve when we work together. ☆

On the FRONT LINES

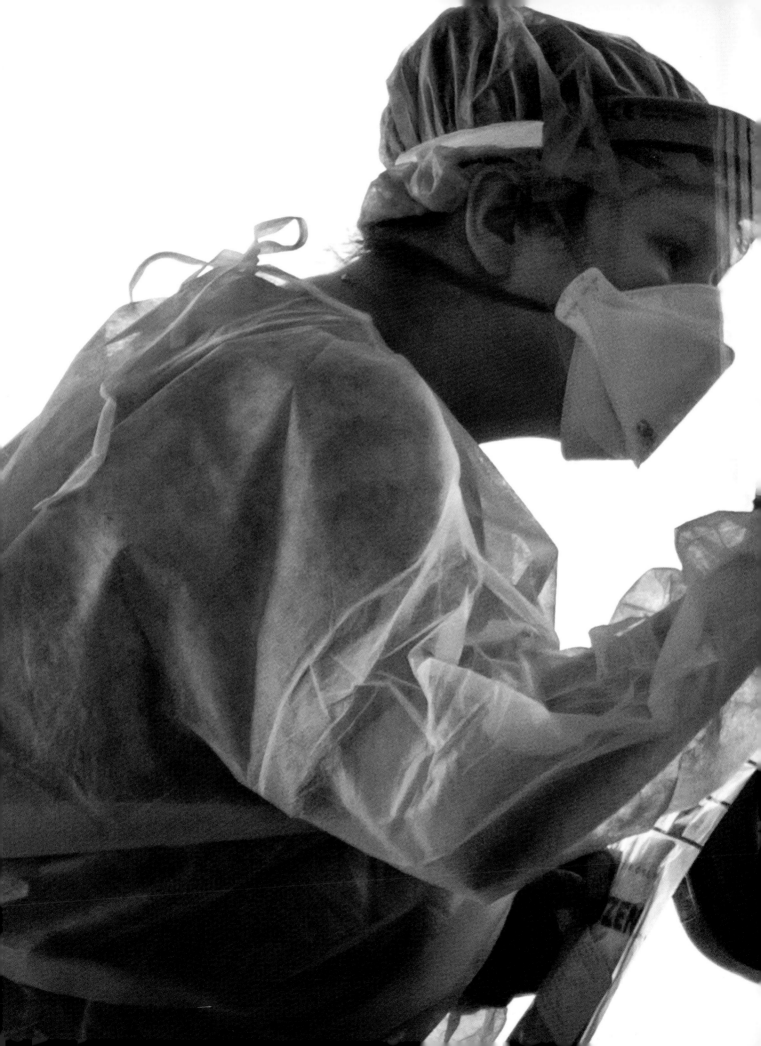

The first line of defense against Covid-19 is testing. Here, a medical professional administers a coronavirus test at a drive-thru testing site run by George Washington University Hospital on May 26, 2020, in Washington, D.C.

Dealing with such a contagious disease means medical workers have to take extreme caution when working with patients. In Yonkers, EMTs clothed in personal protective equipment (PPE) assist a patient into an ambulance. (Inset) In Maryland, PPE was still essential when dealing with a patient in cardiac arrest.

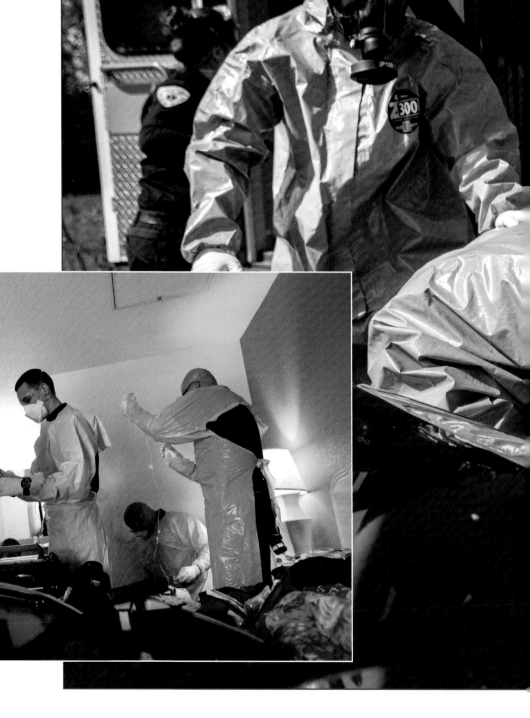

A nurse helps a doctor with his PPE before performing a procedure on a Covid-19 patient in the intensive care unit at Regional Medical Center on May 21, 2020, in San Jose. At the time, Santa Clara county, where this hospital is located, had the most deaths of any Northern California county, and the earliest known Covid-19 related deaths in the United States.

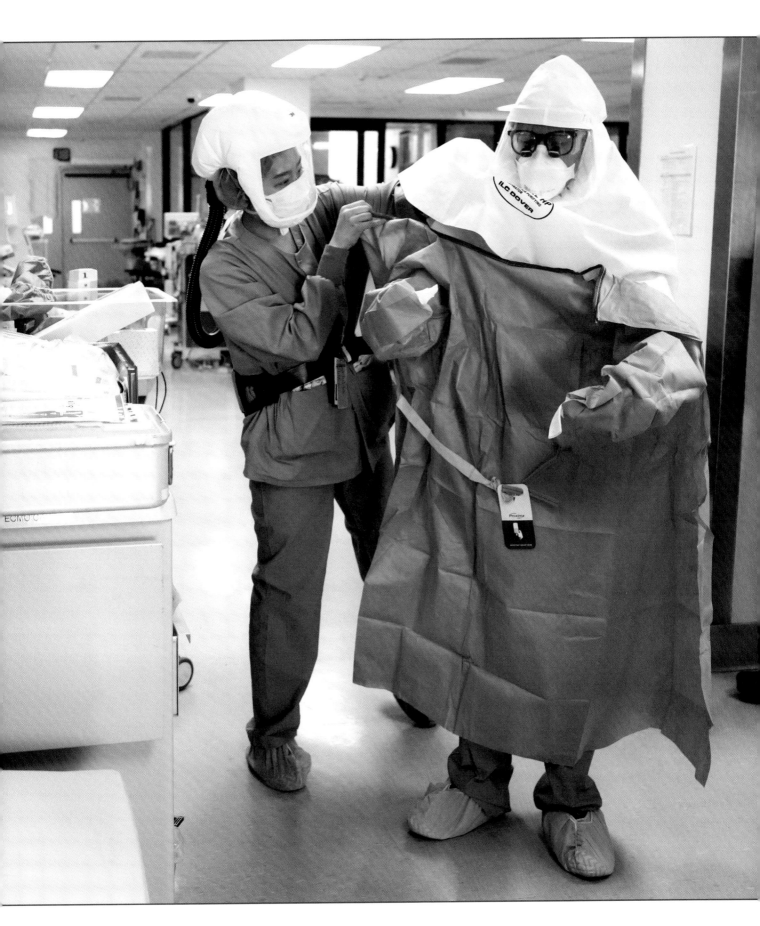

Dr. Natalia Echeverri uses a swab to gather a sample from the noses of Juan Arias and (inset) Silvia Staff, who both said they were homeless, in Miami. Dr. Echeverri is part of a group of community organizations helping the homeless by providing tests, protective masks, gloves, tents, and other items to people in need.

Identifying a possible shortage of respirators, businesses such as Ford Motor Co. began assembling them at their factories. Kyle Lenart (right) inspects a ventilator made in Ypsilanti Township, Michigan. (AP Images) (Inset) Partially assembled bridge ventilators sit at Boyce Technologies Inc. in Long Island City.

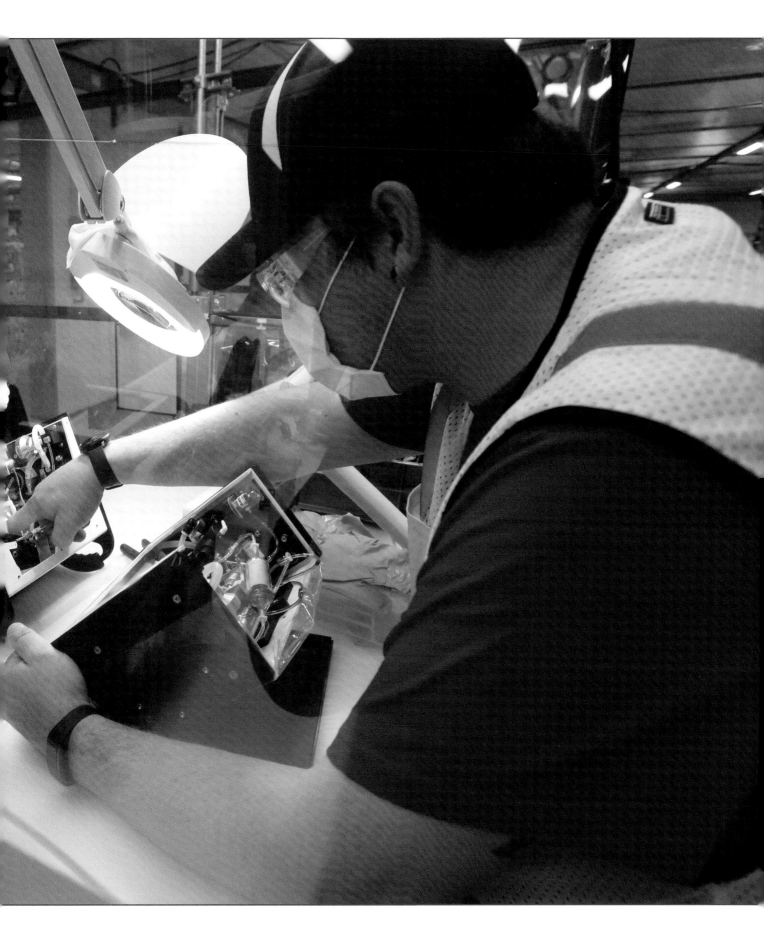

A member of the U.S. Army National Guard hands out food and other essentials at a food pantry in Brooklyn. (Inset) U.S. Army National Guard soldiers distribute food at John Ruiz Park to people suffering from food insecurity in Chelsea, Massachusetts.

The Army Corps of Engineers established a temporary field hospital at Jacob Javits Convention Center in New York City. The site helped eased the burden on New York City hospitals, many of which were overwhelmed with Covid-19 patients.

Medical workers hug outside NYU Langone Hospital as people applaud to show their gratitude to medical staff and essential workers on May 7, 2020, in New York City.

Medical workers and patients know they are in the fight together. Isaias Perez Yanez, 59, is applauded by hospital staff as he is released from Sharp Coronado Hospital after battling Covid-19 for five weeks there in Coronado, California. (Inset) A medical worker hugs a Covid-19 survivor in New York City.

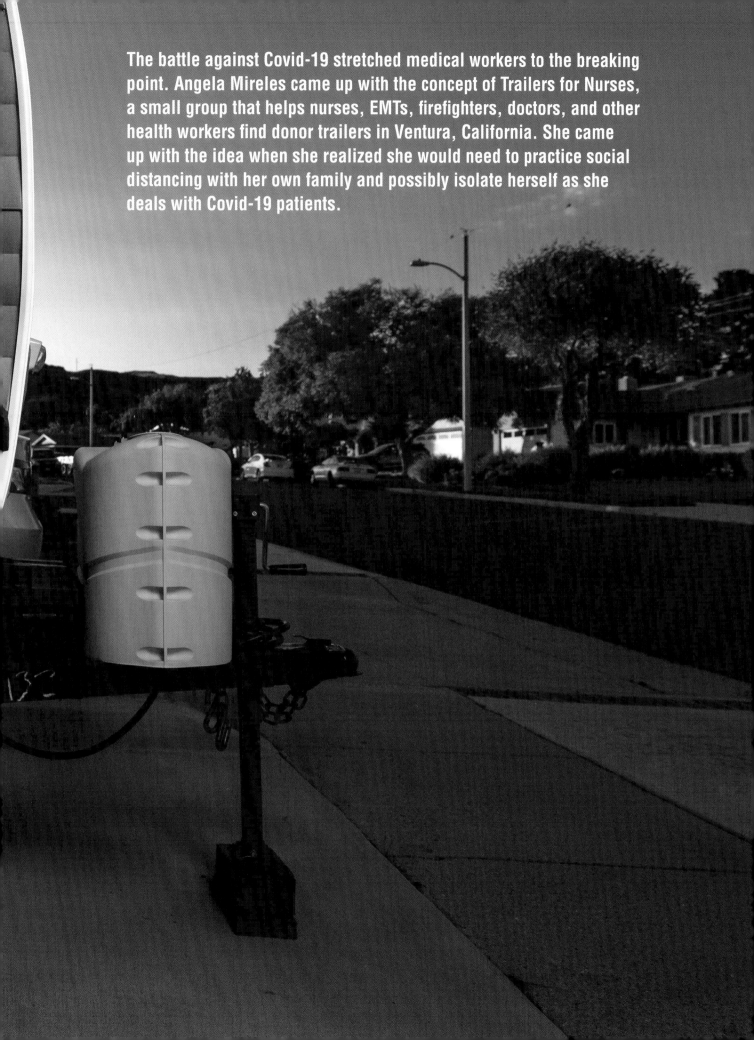

The battle against Covid-19 stretched medical workers to the breaking point. Angela Mireles came up with the concept of Trailers for Nurses, a small group that helps nurses, EMTs, firefighters, doctors, and other health workers find donor trailers in Ventura, California. She came up with the idea when she realized she would need to practice social distancing with her own family and possibly isolate herself as she deals with Covid-19 patients.

In California, police officers and firefighters from across the area lined up outside of Kaiser Hospital in South San Francisco to thank health care workers who are working on the front lines of the pandemic.

Scientists across the country immediately began looking for a vaccine. Dr. Rhonda Flores looks at protein samples at Novavax labs in Gaithersburg, Maryland. (Inset) Farshad Guirakhoo, chief scientific officer at GeoVax, checks on one of the vaccine candidates that his lab is working on in Smyrna, Georgia. (AP Images)

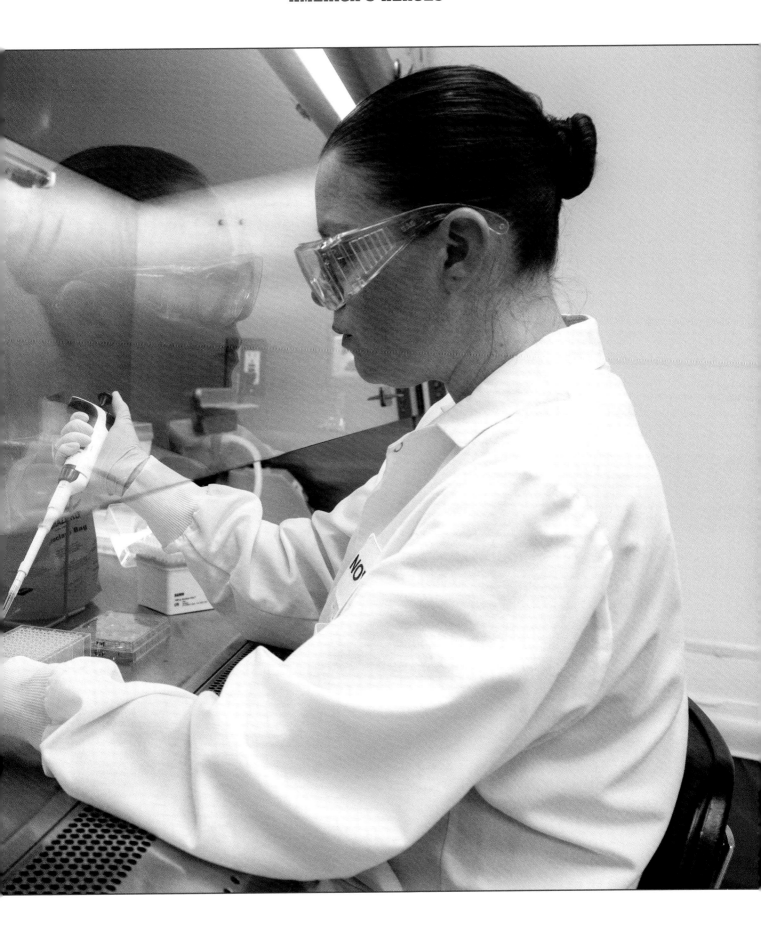

Nurses, doctors, and hospital administrators cheer as the United States Navy Blue Angels pass over Medical City Dallas on May 6, 2020. The flyover was a show of support for health care workers and first responders fighting the pandemic.

Nurses and medical workers pause their work in celebration of Nurse Week and International Nurses Day outside Mt. Sinai Queens on May 12, 2020.

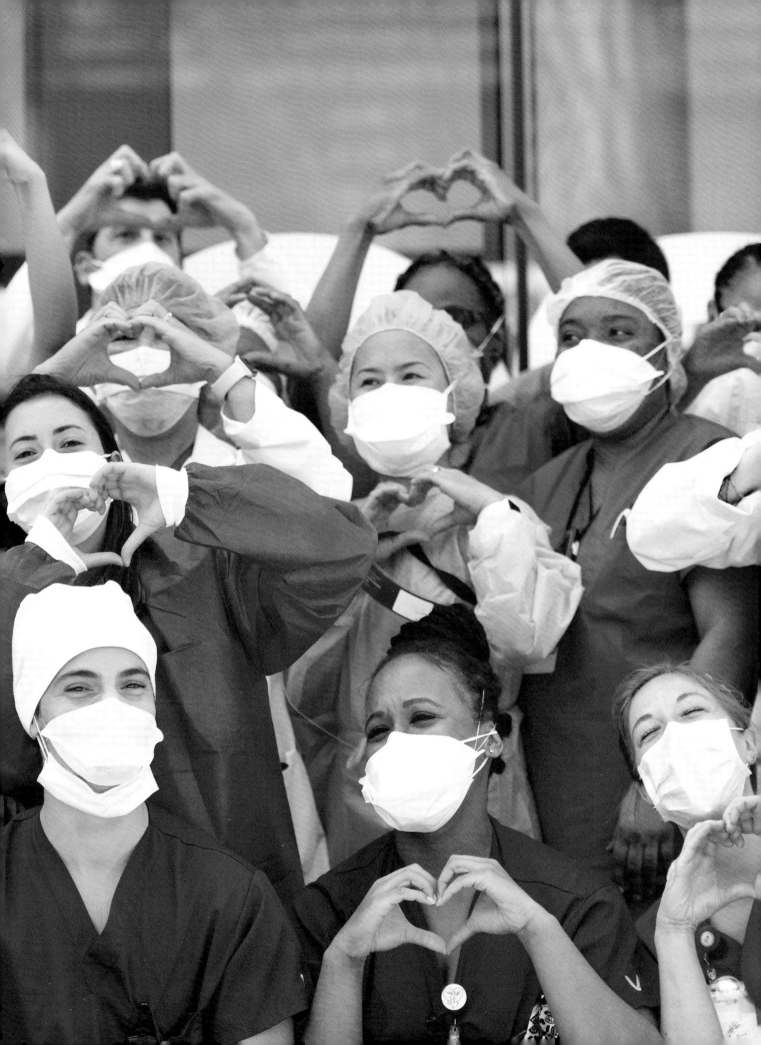

AMERICA AT HOME

One of the cruelest aspects of the pandemic has been isolating ourselves from friends and family. In Wantagh, New York, James Grant could only hug his grandmother, Mary Grace Sileo, through a plastic drop cloth during Memorial Day weekend.

Family members can only watch from outside the room of Isaias Perez Yanez as he is assessed by occupational therapist Jaclyn Lien at Sharp Coronado Hospital in Coronado, California. (Inset) Nurse manager Kate Gouin comforts Fred Castine as his family drives by his nursing home during a parade in Brattleboro, Vermont. (AP Images)

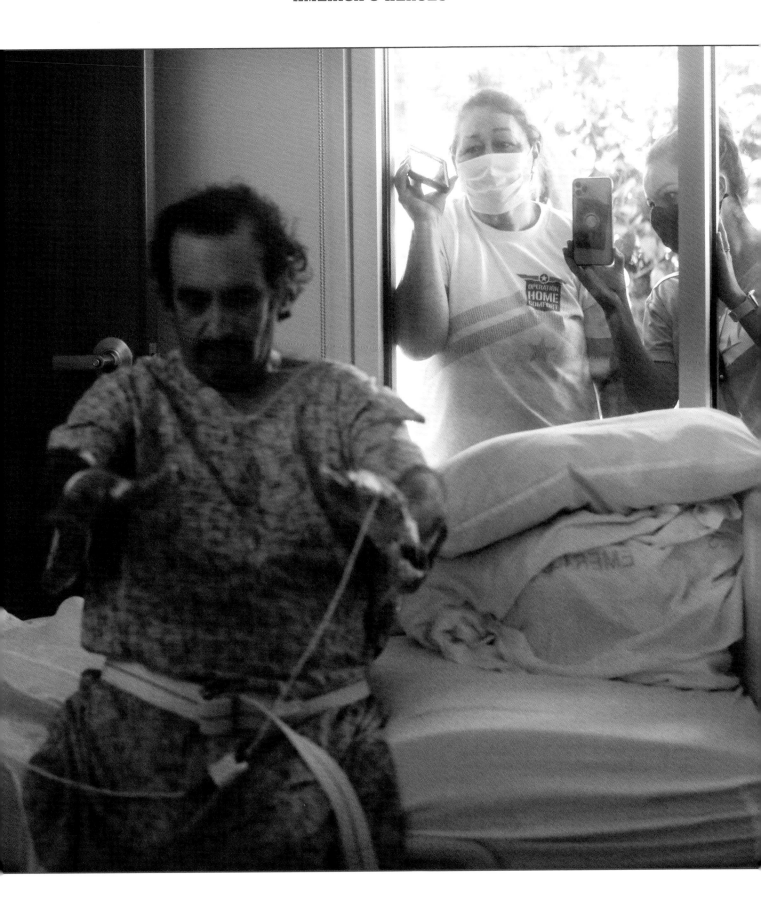

A man rides his bicycle along 7th Avenue through a deserted Times Square on May 21, 2020, in New York City. Approximately 330,000 people pass through Times Square daily; the pandemic temporarily turned it into a ghost town.

Zef Talahun jumps rope in front of the Lincoln Memorial, normally filled with tourists but now nearly empty, on March 17, 2020, in Washington, D.C. (Inset) A view of a desolated Las Vegas Strip in Nevada.

An abandoned South Beach on May 27, 2020, in Miami Beach. (Inset) A virtually empty Los Angeles International Airport on April 16, 2020. Passenger air travel has plummeted more than 90 percent at LAX as airlines canceled flights because of Covid-19.

With houses of worship closed, people demonstrated their faiths in new ways. Yvonne Reiter's bat mitzvah ceremony was moved to her home and broadcast over Zoom in Redmond, Washington. The family had originally planned to have the ceremony at Congregation Beth Shalom in Seattle with a party following of about 100 friends and family at the Seattle Aquarium, before those plans were postponed indefinitely.

Schools closing across the country redirected Americans toward digital learning. A teacher works from her home in Arlington, Virginia, as both educators and students adapted to their new reality. (Inset) The pandemic also turned millions of parents into teachers. Farrah Eaton assists her daughter Elin, 11, with home schooling in New Rochelle, New York. Schools in New Rochelle, a hot spot in the U.S. for Covid-19, were suspended on March 13.

Though video conferencing is not a new technology, the pandemic brought millions of new users to platforms such as Zoom, Microsoft Teams, and Skype. Members of the Vermont House of Representatives convene in a Zoom video conference for its first full parliamentary online session on April 23, 2020. (AP Images) (Inset) The platforms also allowed friends and families to stay connected.

Covid-19 brought many things to a halt, but even it could not stop true love. Couples prepare to take marriage vows at one of six socially distanced marriage booths in the parking lot of the Honda Center on May 19, 2020, in Anaheim. Orange County Clerk-Recorder staff perform the ceremonies from inside the booths and couples are allowed one witness.

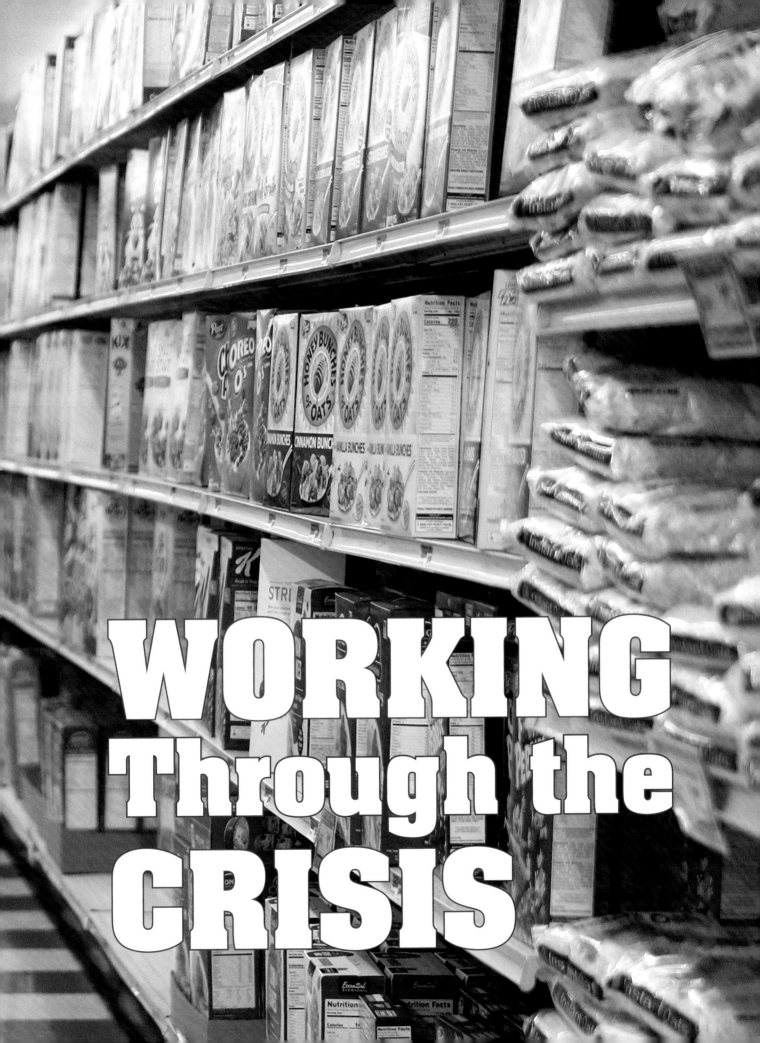

WORKING Through the CRISIS

The employees at Presidente Supermarket in Miami, like the rest of America's grocery store workers, were deemed essential to helping keep the nation fed. Lay Guzman stands behind a partial protective plastic screen and wears a mask and gloves as she works as a cashier.

Millions of Americans came to rely on food delivery services such as Grubhub, DoorDash, and Uber Eats. A Grubhub delivery person is riding a bicycle through an empty street in New York City.

Workers wearing protective masks continued to show up for work and deliver packages across the nation. These UPS workers are loading boxes of N95 respirator masks onto a delivery truck in Louisville on April 13, 2020. (Inset) Samuel Diaz, a delivery worker for Amazon Prime, loads his vehicle with groceries from Whole Foods in Miami. A leap in U.S. unemployment has thrown a spotlight on the gig economy, one type of work still in high demand during the pandemic. (AP Images)

Workers remained committed to keeping America's food supply chain strong. Joe Conte, co-owner of Water2Table Fish Co., readies a hoist for an early-morning delivery of freshly caught local halibut in San Francisco. Conte initially had to lay off his entire staff at the onset of the shutdown after losing all his restaurant contracts, but quickly pivoted to a consumer-based business model and was able to re-hire nearly everyone within a week.

Restaurants, forced to close their doors to diners, instituted curbside and contactless pickup options. A worker waits to serve customers at Emporium Pies in the Bishop Arts District of Dallas. (Inset) A worker delivers food curbside in the Plaza District of Oklahoma City.

Mass transit systems remained critical to people's daily lives; that didn't mean they weren't affected by the pandemic. A Metropolitan Transportation Authority (MTA) cleaning contractor sprays Shockwave RTU disinfectant inside a New York City subway car. The MTA closed the subway system for four hours every night for deep cleaning.

Americans STEP UP

Massive unemployment left many struggling to pay for basic necessities, including food. In Carson, California, cars lined up to receive food distributed by the Los Angeles Regional Food Bank. Around 2,300 families were expected to benefit from the distribution. (Inset) In Brooklyn, lines wrapped around the Barclays Center as people waited to receive food from the Food Bank for New York City.

Allison Bosworth (right) works with her cousin, Adrianne Fiala (left), to operate a farmer's market out of her basement apartment in Brooklyn. The goal is to provide a safer environment for getting food than shopping at a grocery store.

Americans of all ages pitched in wherever they could. Eight-year-old Addison Reed, who comes from a family of potato farmers in Pasco, Washington, gives out free bags of potatoes from growers who, according to Grant Morris of Schneider Farms, are giving away a million pounds of their excess potatoes as a result of the food service industry slowdown. (Inset) A volunteer gives a cyclist two gallons of milk at Boston College High School in Boston. The Dairy Farmers of America donated 8,600 gallons to the milk drive.

Legendary chef Eric Ripert prepares meals for health care workers as part of the World Central Kitchen charity at his flagship New York City restaurant. Hundreds of plastic trays were filled with chicken, rice, and cabbage, a far cry from the usual fare at the famous restaurant Le Bernardin.

The pandemic has inspired an outpouring of "mutual aid," a grassroots form of activism taken up by ordinary Americans. Moné Makkawi uses her bicycle in the Crown Heights neighborhood of Brooklyn to deliver food to New Yorkers in need.

Children who depend on free lunches were in danger of going hungry because of school closures. Dozens of families receive food distributed by Montgomery County Public Schools as part of a program to feed children while schools are closed in Silver Spring, Maryland. (Inset) Christy Cusick hands out free school lunches to kids and their parents at Olympic Hills Elementary School in Seattle.

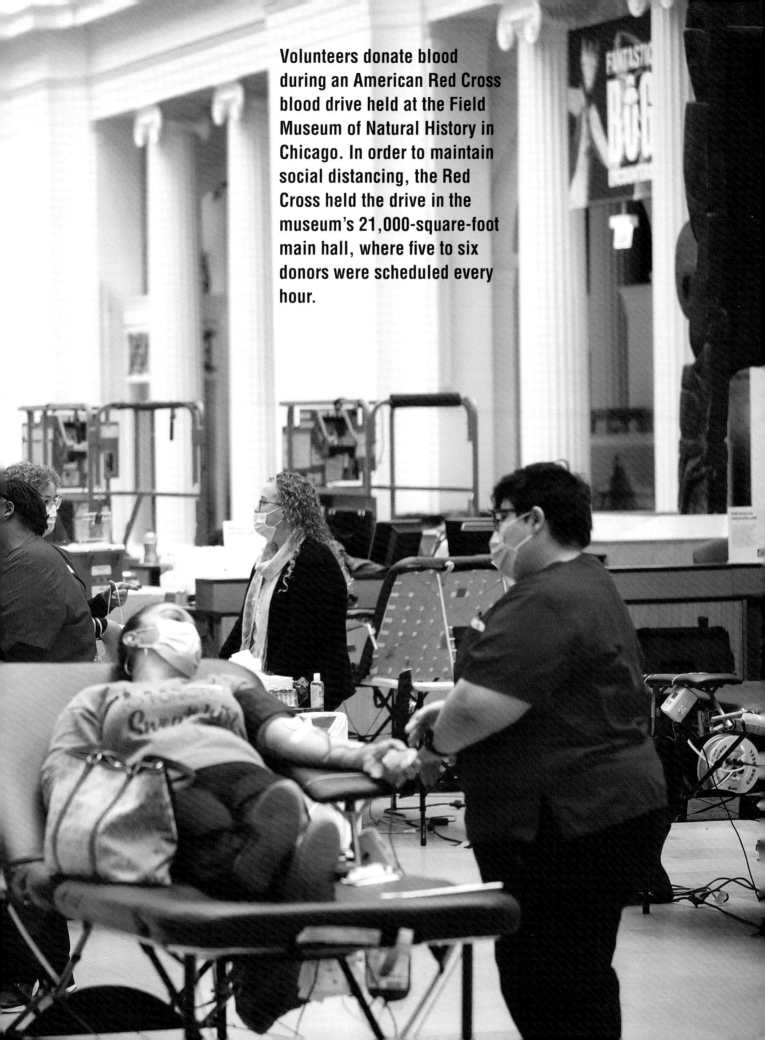

Volunteers donate blood during an American Red Cross blood drive held at the Field Museum of Natural History in Chicago. In order to maintain social distancing, the Red Cross held the drive in the museum's 21,000-square-foot main hall, where five to six donors were scheduled every hour.

A key to battling Covid-19 is keeping our hands clean, and hand sanitizer was occasionally in short supply. The Better Man Distilling Company in Patchogue, New York, transitioned their production from spirits to making hand sanitizer to be distributed to municipalities like the New York Police Department, the United States Postal Service, National Grid, the Patchogue Volunteer Ambulance, and Patchogue Fire Department. (Inset) In Jackson, Mississippi, police officers and a supermarket employee prepare a free hand sanitizer station inside a supermarket.

With everyone in desperate need of face masks and other pieces of PPE, Americans stepped up to make as many as they could. (Clockwise) Jeremy Reitman in Calabasas, California; Meredith Brehm, Ricky Cortez, and Kavita Torres in Maplewood, New Jersey.

Looking to make a difference any way they could, people gathered each night to applaud and support those working on the front lines, cheering from their fire escapes in New York City.

Even during a national emergency, what is life without music? Cellist Jodi Beder performs a daily concert on her front porch in Mount Rainier, Maryland, to help people passing by and her neighbors cope with the pandemic.

With graduation ceremonies canceled across the country, celebrities including Alicia Keys and (inset) Nick Jonas donated their time to Graduate America, a television and online special designed to congratulate the class of 2020.

Sports and Entertainment Take Timeout

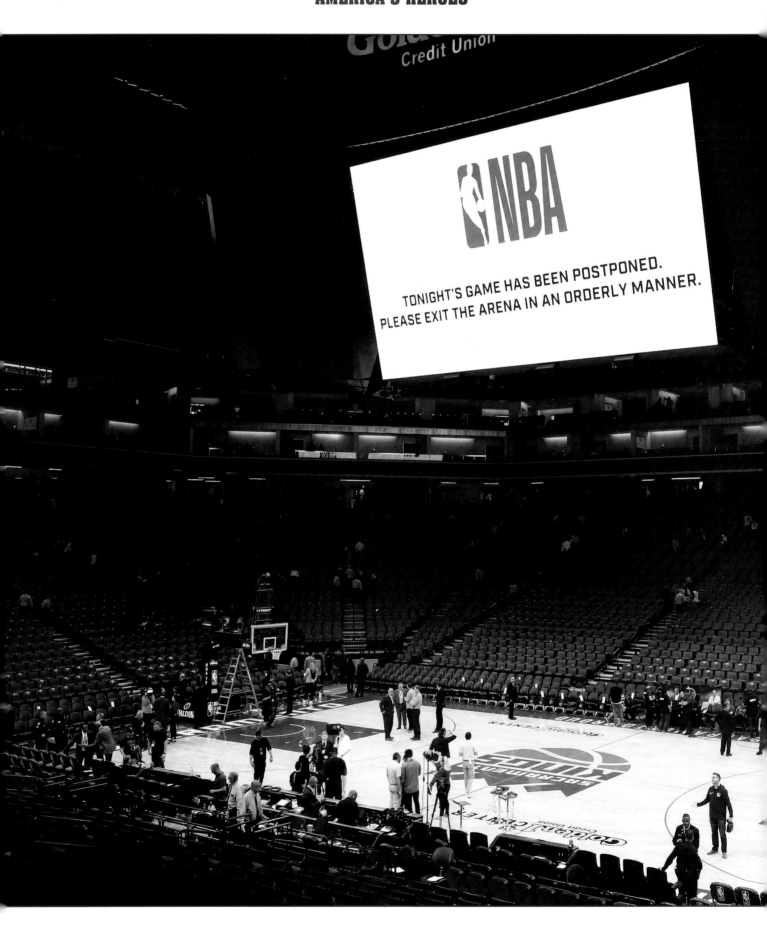

One of the first indications that Covid-19 would dramatically change our lives was the suspension of the NBA season on the night of March 11, 2020. After Utah Jazz center Ruby Gobert tested positive for the coronavirus, that night's game between the New Orleans Pelicans and Sacramento Kings was canceled.

Opening day of the baseball season is a date many look forward to each year; not so in 2020. Both Wrigley Field and Fenway Park showed their support for medical workers and those forced to stay home because of Covid-19.

Chicago's United Center, home to the Bulls and Blackhawks, was transformed into a staging area for food items to be delivered to those in need. (AP Images)

Just because the Summer Olympics were canceled didn't mean our athletes stopped training. Fencer Katharine Holmes trains with her boyfriend, Tyler Christensen, during a training session at her home in Princeton, New Jersey. The epee fencer was training anywhere from 6-8 hours a day at Princeton University before the pandemic, but now continues that intense regimen at home.

Phil Mickelson, Tom Brady, Peyton Manning, and Tiger Woods participated in The Match: Champions for Charity at Medalist Golf Club in Hobe Sound, Florida. The foursome squared off in the televised exhibition match and raised $20 million for Covid-19 relief efforts.

With movie theaters closed, some Americans rediscovered the joy of the drive-in movie, including this couple watching *The Rocky Horror Picture Show* in an improvised theatre in Queens. (AP Images) (Inset) In Fort Smith, Arkansas, Travis McCready held a socially-distanced concert at TempleLive on May 18, 2020.

Americans may have been asked to stay home, but the same wasn't always true of animals. In Kansas City, penguins from the Kansas City Zoo took a field trip to the Nelson-Atkins Museum of Art and wandered through the exhibits. Video of the penguins' day out was watched hundreds of thousands of times. (AP Images)

Global Citizen's One World: Together at Home virtual concert brought together some of the biggest names in entertainment, such as the Rolling Stones, (insets) Lady Gaga, and Oprah Winfrey. The benefit was broadcast across a number of networks and streaming platforms, and raised nearly $130 million for Covid-19 relief efforts.

OPRAH WINFREY

A New Dawn

Longing for fresh air and a feeling of community, Americans went outdoors as safely as they could. In Brooklyn's Domino Park, white circles were painted on the grass to help people maintain social distancing.

In June, Yosemite National Park reopened, allowing visitors to walk toward the Tunnel View lookout. Only about half of the average June visitors will be allowed in, and they must make an online reservation for each car.

Partitions were erected in Boston to separate restaurant patrons set up on the sidewalk, after the city gave temporary permission for restaurants to use public streets and sidewalks for outdoor seating. (AP Images) (Inset) Customers try out social distancing devices made of rubber tubing at Fish Tales Bar & Grill in Ocean City, Maryland.

People drink outdoor at bars and restaurants in the Hell's Kitchen neighborhood of New York City on June 7, 2020, as the city entered phase one of the state's plan to reboot economic activities.

One of the first sports to return to competition has been auto racing. Daniel Hemric, driver of the #8 Poppy Bank Chevrolet, stands for the national anthem prior to the NASCAR Xfinity Series EchoPark 250 at Atlanta Motor Speedway on June 6, 2020, in Hampton, Georgia.

E'RE STRONG.

Covid-19 has tested our collective will physically, economically, and emotionally. But it has also proven once again that America is stronger when we stand together.